OUTSOURCING UNLEASHED

Outsourcing Unleashed

A Comprehensive Guide to Business Expansion

Jim Stephens

QuantumQuill Press

CONTENTS

The Publisher has made every effort to ensure that this report is as precise and thorough as feasible. However, it is crucial to acknowledge that the Publisher neither guarantees nor makes any representations regarding the accuracy of the contents at any moment, as a result of the Internet's dynamic nature.

Although the Publisher has diligently attempted to verify the information in this publication, any errors, omissions, or contrary interpretations of the subject matter shall not be held liable. Any perceived slights directed at particular organizations, individuals, or peoples are unintentional.

Practical advice books, similar to other domains, do not provide assurances of financial gain. Readers are advised to exercise their own discernment with respect to their specific situations and to take appropriate action in response.

It is imperative to underscore that this literary work should not be regarded as a substitute for legal, business, accountancy, or financial counsel. It is highly recommended that all readers retain the expertise of proficient experts in the domains of law, business, accountancy, and finance.

1

INTRODUCTION

Amidst the current surge in the prominence of home-based enterprises, the notion of outsourcing has also garnered significant attention. Those who are seeking to revolutionize their home-based enterprises frequently resort to outsourcing as a means to engage competent professionals in collaboration.

Concurrently, even the most sizable organizations are progressively delegating substantial portions of their operations to international specialists. The extensive implementation of outsourcing would not have taken place in the absence of significant advantages linked to it.

This book explores the strategies for outsourcing that can substantially increase the productivity of a business.

2

WHY ENGAGE IN OUTSOURCING?

Prior to recent years, outsourcing was not a particularly popular practice. Indeed, there was widespread reluctance among individuals to acknowledge that they were outsourcing their work due to the widespread belief that doing so indicated incompetence and that the quality of the work would undoubtedly suffer. Nevertheless, circumstances have evolved. In contemporary times, outsourcing has not only gained immense popularity but has also become an almost standard practice for organizations. Owing to the proliferation of home-based enterprises, outsourcing has attained its pinnacle of popularity. In any case, how could an individual operating from their residence effectively handle every business-related obligation without resorting to the services of freelancers to whom they could delegate their tasks?

Consider the following as the primary justifications for outsourcing your business:

1.Utilizing the assistance of a group of experts, increase your workload by collaborating with an extensive variety of customers.

2.Enhance team diversity by enlisting the services of outsourcing experts possessing a range of credentials and proficiencies; this will enable you to undertake assignments that you may have otherwise shied away from on account of your own constraints.

3.Manage business-related duties in which you may lack expertise or enthusiasm; in this case, outsourcing is a highly effective solution for achieving these objectives.

4.You can enhance your capacity to meet deadlines by outsourcing.

5.By delegating tasks to specialists in regions where particular services are more affordable, you can reduce expenses. A considerable number of individuals delegate tasks from developed to developing nations, utilizing economic disparities as an opportunity to cut costs and adhere to stricter financial constraints.

Most significantly, the feeling of isolation can be overpowering when working remotely, particularly when confronted with critical decision-making processes. Having highly knowledgeable experts on your team facilitates the execution of these tasks.

3

WHICH VARIETIES OF WORK MAY BE OUTSOURCED?

Every business, from small home-based operations to large corporate ventures, entails an extensive array of responsibilities. Although the intricacy is readily apparent in larger organizations, even home-based businesses involve a multitude of processes, including but not limited to financing, investment acquisition, task management, communication, payment processing, and task identification. Prospective home business owners are confronted with an extensive array of obligations. Consequently, which duties become amenable to outsourcing?

With the financial means, it is possible to locate professionals in our Internet-enabled, interconnected world who can assist with a variety of duties, including the strategic planning of entire business ventures. However, particularly when initially on a tight budget, it is prudent to outsource only those tasks that you truly are unable to complete internally. Implementing a strategy of outsourcing certain facets of business execution is a judicious course of action. For instance, in the case where your home-based enterprise is predicated on producing written content, you might opt to delegate the writing component to an external entity. Nevertheless, crucial elements including strategizing, procuring clients, communicating with them, processing payments, and so forth, ought to remain under your jurisdiction. Certain individuals procure work at elevated rates and remunerate the writers they outsource to with a fixed fee, thus generating the surplus funds.

For a variety of factors, outsourcing the execution portion of your project is advantageous:

· The most laborious task is frequently the execution phase. For example, in the case of operating a website design and development company, the most arduous aspect is undoubtedly the website design process. You are able to concentrate on acquiring additional customers while this task is being outsourced.

· Your control over the execution phase is enhanced. You can evaluate the quality of content written by your employees and, if necessary, return it for proofreading or altering. Likewise, you retain overall oversight when someone else designs a logo for your client, allowing you to review the work and propose modifications.

Your company will almost certainly require more outsourcing services as it expands. One might need the services of a data entry specialist to uphold organizational records, a communicator to provide regular updates to clients regarding progress, or a manager to oversee the tendering process and other work acquisition methods. Experts in outsourcing are accessible to address a variety of requirements, spanning from comprehensive business management to telemarketing. The crucial factor is recognizing when to effectively employ these professionals.

4

LOCATING QUALIFIED INDIVIDUALS TO OUTSOURCE YOUR TASKS TO

If you are considering outsourcing your work needs, consider the following advice regarding how to locate qualified professionals:

Internet-based job platforms

Online employment boards are the most efficient method for locating outsourcing specialists. The following are ten of the finest websites:

1.Obtain a Freelancer

2.Literal Lance

3.Freelance EU

4.The eLance

5.Guru

6.Rental-A Coder

7.Humans Per Hour

8.The Exchange of Lime

9.The oDesk

10.Acquire anoder

You can post your project in one of the numerous job categories on these websites, and qualified professionals will submit bids. The uncomplicated notion guarantees that you will establish connections with individuals who are legitimately in search of employment.

Discussion forums

Numerous online forums serve as platforms for project postings and proposals. Although a bidding component is present, it is not as prevalent as it is on freelance job boards. The prominent forum Digital Point Forums (http://forum.digitalpoint.com/) is a resource for locating individuals to manage your initiatives.

5

NETWORKING SOCIAL MEDIA WEBSITES

One may utilize any social networking site as a resource to locate professionals. Prominent online platforms such as MySpace (http://www.myspace.com), Facebook (http://www.facebook.com), and Twitter (http://www.twitter.com) host groups catering to freelance professionals. By becoming a member of these groups, you are granted access to publish your initiatives.

Conversely, work-related activities might not be accorded due importance on social networking sites, and there is a lack of established safeguards to secure individuals collaborating, as is evident on freelance job sites that utilize escrow systems.

6

ACQUIRING EXPERTS VIA ONLINE JOB BOARDS

Online employment boards are the preeminent locations to establish connections with industry experts; therefore, we shall further explore their benefits:

1.Intent to Work: Participants on construction sites have enrolled with the explicit intention of securing employment. Although certain job sites offer free memberships, others demand payment, a practice that frequently indicates members' greater professionalism and sincerity.

2.A rating and review system is implemented at every jobsite, catering to the needs of both employees and employers. This functionality enables users to evaluate the credentials and standing of a specific employee, thereby facilitating well-informed decision-making.

3.Escrow System: An escrow system is implemented on every jobsite to efficiently manage and resolve any conflicts that may emerge throughout the course of the project. This ensures that disputes between parties are resolved fairly.

4.Detailed Project Posts: Project requirements, timeline, and budget can be outlined in detail in detailed project posts. The subsequent response from bidders obviates the necessity for subsequent negotiations.

5.Sample Requests: Prospective candidates may be required to submit samples of their previous work, which will offer valuable insights into their capabilities and appropriateness for the given undertaking.

6.By actively inviting individuals to submit bids on your project, you will increase the number of qualified candidates.

The procedure for posting projects on online job boards is uncomplicated. Free project postings are permitted on platforms such as GetAFreelancer in exchange for a nominal refundable deposit. Simply provide all required information, including a timeline and budget, and submit the assignment in the appropriate category.

As soon as your project goes live, tendering commences immediately. The objective is to thoroughly evaluate the proposals and arrive at a well-informed judgment regarding the candidate most qualified for the project. Although direct communication with bidders is limited until the selection process is complete, a private message board enables interaction in accordance with predetermined guidelines, thereby assisting in the making of decisions.

Numerous individuals are forging enduring and fruitful professional relationships via these online freelance job platforms, surmounting geographical limitations in the process while benefiting from one another's expertise. By virtue of their virtual nature, these interactions enable employers and professionals to collaborate efficiently and affordably, without the requirement of physical proximity.

7

CHOOSING THE APPROPRIATE PERSON

Several factors should be taken into account when selecting an outsourcing professional from freelance job boards such as GetAFreelancer, ScriptLance, or oDesk in order to ensure that you make the best decision.

To begin with, clarity is crucial. Precisely delineate every aspect of the project, encompassing the subsequent elements in your project post:

- The characteristics of your labor
- The overall quantity of labor
- Milestones, delineating whether the work is to be executed in phases or within a specified period of time;
- The total time allotted for the completion of the assignment
- The amount of money that you are prepared to expend
- Any particular attributes that you are actively pursuing in personnel

· Qualities of personnel that you hold in high regard or wish to be absent

Special factors that are essential for making decisions, such as samples.

Publish the project in the appropriate category to ensure that it reaches the intended audience. Applicants are notified in accordance with the categories they have submitted applications for; therefore, if you submit your project in the incorrect category, it may fail to reach its intended audience.

Providing comprehensive project information improves the probability of attracting qualified professionals to submit bids for your endeavor. Although you might receive a reduced number of proposals, it is probable that they will surpass expectations in quality.

Examine samples of their work thoroughly, as this will constitute a pivotal criterion in your assessment. Specify in your project posting whether an original sample is required; individuals who are willing to contribute one will do so.

Assemble the employee's trust by commencing the collaboration with a brief-term undertaking. Once trust has been established, longer-term endeavors can be considered.

Select professionals according to the subsequent criteria:

· The evident quality of their work as demonstrated by their samples.

· Accumulated ratings and evaluations on the website.

· Promptness, with an emphasis on the value of timely email replies and, ideally, the possession of an instant messaging identification.

· The pricing aspect should be considered, but it should not be the exclusive determinant, unless one is operating under a strict financial constraint.

After locating a reputable expert, guarantee timely remuneration and furnish an evaluation predicated on their performance. This promotes a constructive professional rapport, thereby diminishing the necessity for iterative employee searches.

8

THE MONEY EQUATION AND OUTSOURCING: DETERMINING HOW MUCH TO PAY AND HOW

Monetary considerations are fundamental to all business relationships, given that they are the reason for the very existence of the enterprise. Consequently, it is critical to accurately calculate the monetary equation.

One of the benefits of utilizing the Internet to locate outsourcing professionals is the wide range of financial resources that are accessible. Individuals submit bids for your projects, allowing you to select them according to your financial means. Establish an approximation of your budget; the vast majority of proposals will fit within this range.

It is possible to locate competent professionals willing to work within your budget! It is important to bear in mind that you are conducting business in a global marketplace, where wages for employees in other nations can vary substantially from what is customary in your region.

Diverse occupations exhibit distinct financial dynamics. Preliminary bids on low-budget projects serve as a viable means to assess the proficiency of a professional. Inform them that payments will be evaluated in accordance with the caliber of their work. This methodology not only enables one to evaluate the professional's aptitudes but also sustains their motivation through the promise of increased compensation.

Before submitting your project to a job board, investigate comparable projects that have been submitted by other users. This offers valuable understanding regarding the current payment norms. Nevertheless, it is imperative to maintain a personal budget in mind while composing your project post.

Escrows are

In the outsourcing equation, escrows are indispensable, and they provide advantages for employers and employees alike. Additional elaboration on escrows will be addressed in the following chapter.

Digital Banks

PayPal (http://www.paypal.com) is widely recognized as the preeminent online banking platform utilized by freelance outsourcers. A close competitor is Moneybookers, which can be found at http://www.moneybookers.com/. It is recommended that individuals who frequently outsource maintain a Payoneer debit card (http://www.payoneer.com/), given that it is affiliated with the majority of freelance job boards, such as GetAFreelancer, ScriptLance, and oDesk.

No fees are assessed when funds are transferred from these websites to the Payoneer debit card.

Escrows and Milestones Outsourced

The importance of milestones and escrows in attracting top-tier professionals for your projects cannot be exaggerated. In the context of extensive undertakings, milestones assume a pivotal function by facilitating the delivery of deliverables in feasible installments. We are aware, as was previously stated, of the significance of escrows.

Specific websites, such as eLance, provide functionalities that enable users to define the format they desire their deliverables to be in. The establishment of project milestones, which is made possible by platforms such as eLance, offers numerous benefits. This procedure guarantees that the employee is in a more effective position to handle deadlines, while also affording you increased supervision of the project.

It is recommended to commence with short-term assignments until a rapport has been established with the employee. Notwithstanding the apparent seamlessness of the tendering process, complications may manifest throughout the course of the project. Short-term initiatives provide increased adaptability and a more straightforward method of withdrawing in the event of complications. The minimum value requirement for posting a project on GetAFreelancer is $30, whereas the majority of other platforms do not impose such restrictions.

The escrow system is considered the most favorable form of payment. The fact that escrows protect both parties is a significant advantage of these freelance platforms, which are implemented on the majority of job sites. After a purchaser has been chosen, funds are deposited into an escrow account. The website retains this sum and withholds its release to the purchaser until the completion of the task.

Escrows offer numerous advantages. If, in the future, complications with the project prevent you from releasing payment, you may request that the website arbitrate. Generally, freelance websites refrain from engaging in arbitration in the absence of an established escrow. Moreover, the employee's knowledge that funds have been allocated for the undertaking serves as an incentive to produce a work of superior quality.

Ratings, reviews, and relationships are the three Rs that maintain the outsourcing tide.

Critical to a sustainable outsourcing solution is the development of a lasting rapport with a dependable employee. An examination of the complexities associated with the utilization of freelance outsource professionals uncovers the obstacles that are at play. It demands diligence, devotion, excellence, originality, and equitable pricing. Obtaining productive work from an individual whose geographical or social standing you are unfamiliar with or have little knowledge of is not always assured.

After securing the services of a proficient professional, it is imperative to prioritize their retention on the payroll of your outsourcing organization. The following are three essential Rs to bear in mind:

Ratings

You are available to provide a rating for the professional upon completion of a designated task. Certain forums also employ a ten-star rating system, which is utilized by the majority of freelance websites. Remember to give the employee a rating for their outstanding performance. It is more beneficial to evaluate individuals based on their positive contributions rather than their deficiencies. A person is likely to feel valued and motivated to engage in further collaboration if they produce outstanding work and obtain a favorable evaluation.

An analysis of

Reviews serve a comparable purpose to ratings, albeit with greater specificity, enabling users to articulate their opinions verbally. You possess the liberty to express your thoughts and opinions openly, emphasizing elements that you found valuable. Regarding outsourcing professionals, ratings and evaluations carry substantial importance, comparable to an offline professional boasting exceptional accomplishments on their curriculum vitae.

Involvements in relationships

Establishing a cordial and candid relationship with an expert who has demonstrated their competence is a prudent course of action. It is important to consider that your need for them may outweigh their need for you, given the ample job prospects that are accessible to them. Adhering to an informal and congenial mode of communication can yield advantageous outcomes. Boundaries may need to be established on occasion; however, they should be implemented in a subtle and constructive manner.

Completing Your Job Duties

There is no reason why the desired results cannot be obtained if the guidelines have been diligently adhered to thus far. Nevertheless, obstacles might materialize, and it is of the utmost importance to resolve them expeditiously.

The absence of response time is a concern that demands zero tolerance. The unspoken norm on the internet stipulates that a response to any professional email should be received within twenty-four hours, or earlier if mutually agreed upon. A 24-hour delay is superfluous if you are situated in the same time zone. In the absence of responses within the designated timeframe, it is prudent to initiate an investigation into alternative courses of action.

Wherever possible, quality should be prioritized. Monitoring the progress of your outsourcing professional is crucial, even if they have consistently produced high-quality work. Given the absence of face-to-face interaction, it is conceivable that certain individuals may delegate the tasks to less expensive resources, thereby leading to a deterioration in the overall quality. Ensure direct communication with the individual performing the work when outsourcing; avoid using intermediaries.

Often, individuals serve as the most suitable outsourcing professionals for home-based enterprises. Companies ought to be circumvented unless it is absolutely essential. When a sizable organization is in need of services such as telemarketing, it may be necessary to assemble a group of experts.

Even with meticulous professional selection, two significant issues that may arise are a lack of response time and a deterioration in quality. It is imperative that these concerns are not allowed to persist, as they have the potential to greatly affect your organization.

Maintaining a cordial relationship with your professionals is not only vital, but essential, provided that they consistently produce high-quality work. When the professional dimension of the relationship starts to decline, it becomes imperative to adopt a more authoritative position. Allow your inner "boss" to manifest itself when the occasion demands it.

9

ELEVATING THE PRACTICE OF OUTSOURCING: A CRITICAL DEVELOPMENT IN THE EVOLUTION OF ONLINE BUSINESSES

After establishing a solid rapport with the outsourcing professional you encountered on a freelance work platform, you should proceed to contemplate more enduring agreements. Since establishing long-lasting professional relationships is mutually beneficial, some businesses choose to construct contracts and agreements in order to avoid the trouble of repeatedly hiring outsourcing professionals.

Prior to being returned, these documents are delivered to the professional's address and necessitate their signature.

Contracts provide mutual protection, thereby promoting more robust professional collaborations. The establishment of a contract obviates the necessity for repetitive searches for outsourcing professionals. In the same way, a professional who has a stable clientele is better able to concentrate on providing consistent results that meet your expectations.

Unexpectedly, many relationships that commence informally via the internet progress into outsourcing professionals becoming permanent employees of thriving corporations they formerly worked for, sometimes even in different countries. These individuals possess considerable worth for the organizations as they have observed their development since its inception, thereby cultivating a perception of confidence and reliance.

Consequently, proceed immediately with outsourcing to its next level. One or more devoted and effective business allies who are committed to your long-term success may be among those you encounter.

To conclude,

The current business landscape is dominated by outsourcing, and you should unquestionably employ this tactic to expand your company's operations. There is a suitable outsourcing professional for every business need. Having acquired the requisite understanding to effectively locate and retain them, I extend my sincerest wishes for continued success in your pursuits.